D0719673

GALWAY COUNTY LIBRARIES

USING
SCIENCE
BE A VOLCANOLOGIST

By Suzy Gazlay

Volcanology Consultant: Robert B. Trombley PhD

Series Consultant: Kirk A. Janowiak

ticktock

GALWAY COUNTY LIBRARIES

USING
SCIENCE
BE A VOLCANOLOGIST

By Suzy Gazlay
Consultant: Robert B. Trombley Ph.D.
Series consultant: Kirk A. Janowiak
ticktock project editors: Jo Hanks and Joe Harris
ticktock designer: James Powell
With thanks to: Sara Greasley and Anna Brett

Copyright © ticktock Entertainment Ltd 2008
First published in Great Britain in 2008 by ticktock Media Ltd.,
Unit 2, Orchard Business Centre, North Farm Road, Tunbridge Wells, Kent, TN2 3XF

ISBN 978 1 84696 617 0 pbk
ISBN 978 1 84696 679 8 hbk

Printed in China

J245.120 £18.50
GALWAY COUNTY LIBRARIES

A CIP catalogue record for this book is available from the British Library.
All rights reserved. No part of this publication may be reproduced, copied, stored in a retrieval system
or transmitted in any form or by any means electronic, mechanical, photocopying, recording or otherwise without
prior written permission of the copyright owner.

SUZY GAZLAY

Suzy Gazlay (MA Integrated Math/Science Education) is a teacher and writer who has worked with students of all ages. She has also served as a science specialist, curriculum developer, and consultant in varying capacities. She is the recipient of a Presidential Award for Excellence in Math and Science Teaching. Now retired from fulltime classroom teaching, she continues to write, consult, and work with educators and children, particularly in science and music education.
Her many interests include music, environmental issues, marine biology, and the outdoors.

KIRK A. JANOWIAK

BS Biology & Natural Resources, MS Ecology & Animal Behavior, MS Science Education. Kirk has enjoyed teaching students from preschool through to college age. He has been awarded the National Association of Biology Teachers' Outstanding Biology Teacher Award and was honoured to be a finalist for the Presidential Award for Math and Science Teaching. Kirk currently teaches Biology and Environmental Science and enjoys a wide range of interests from music to the art of roasting coffee.

ROBERT B. TROMBLEY PhD

Principal Research Volcanologist of the International Volcano Research Centre and a registered volcanologist. He is an award-winning scientist and has spent 42 years in the field. 'RB' has written several papers and authored two books. He has also written several articles for various volcano related publications. Dr Trombley has also served as a Technical Advisor to the National Geographic Society on a TV documentary about volcanoes. Dr Trombley is a Professor Emeritus at the Phoenix, Arizona campus of the DeVry University.

CONTENTS

This book supports the teaching of science at Key Stage 2 of the National Curriculum. Students will develop their understanding of these areas of scientific inquiry:

- Ideas and evidence in science
- Investigative skills
- Obtaining and presenting evidence
- Considering and evaluating evidence

Students will also learn about:

- The elements of a volcano
- Different types of volcanoes
- How lava is classified
- The Volcanic Explosivity Index (VEI)
- Earth's layers
- Tectonic plate movement
- The Ring of Fire
- Instruments used to predict eruptions
- Volcanic gases
- How earthquake vibrations are measured
- Mudflows and lahars
- Varieties of tephra (volcanic rock)
- Ash clouds and pyroclastic flows
- Soil fertility after an eruption

HOW TO USE THIS BOOK

Science is important in the lives of people everywhere. We use science at home and at school. In fact, we use it all the time. Everybody needs to know about science to understand how the world works. A volcanologist needs to understand geology. This is the science of how Earth is put together. They use this science to try to tell when a volcano will erupt, and to protect us from the dangers of an eruption. With this book you will get the chance use science to follow a volcanic eruption.

This exciting science book is very easy to use — check out what's inside!

INTRODUCTION

Fun to read information about being a volcanologist.

FACTFILE

Easy to understand information about how geology works.

EYEWITNESS TO AN ERUPTION

The eruption has started. It is stunning. You hold your breath as you watch. But you are also very busy working with the data as it comes in. The sights and sounds of the eruption surround you as you go about your work. You measure, record, and take pictures even as you are caught up in the spectacular events unfolding around you. Everyone in the lab will be very busy for a while.

FACTFILE

The volcano erupts with a huge blast.

- One side of the mountain collapses, releasing pressure.
- The natural dam of a lake cracks and then crumbles.
- A flood of water from the lake spills down the side of the mountain and mixes with hot ash. A lahar is set in motion.
- The lahar picks up rock debris as it races downhill, gaining speed.

Some buildings are carried away by the mudflow, while others are buried.

WORKSTATION

Real life volcanology experiences, situations and problems for you to read about.

WORKSTATION

This volcano is blasting out a huge amount of tephra. The ash is rising and blowing away. The rest is raining down all around the volcano.

- Ash is the smallest kind of tephra. It ranges from very fine to rather coarse grains.

- Lapilli are fragments that are larger than a pea but smaller than a walnut. They look like cinders.

- Blocks are larger chunks of rock with angular sides. They were solid when they were blown out of the volcano.

- Bombs were molten lava when they were shot from the volcano. They cooled quickly as they flew through the air, so they have a rounded, streamlined shape.

- Tephra can be deadly. During and after an eruption, ash can fill the air, making it difficult to breathe. Some cities have been buried as much as three metres deep.

- Pumice is a volcanic rock. It is very light in weight because it is full of holes. The holes were formed by gases expanding as erupting lava cooled.

IF YOU NEED HELP!

TIPS FOR SCIENCE SUCCESS

On page 30 you will find lots of tips to help you with your science work.

ANSWERS

Turn to page 31 to check your answers. (*Try all the activities and questions before you take a look at the answers.*)

GLOSSARY

On page 32 there is a glossary of volcanology and science words.

Q CHALLENGE QUESTIONS

Through the eruption, you take photographs. These will go in the lab's permanent records.

1. Which type of tephra is so small and light that it can ride the wind for hundreds of kilometres?

2. The volcano spits out jagged chunks of rock more than 30 centimetres wide. What type of tephra are they?

3. You find a chunk of volcanic rock which is so lightweight that it floats. What is it called?

4. You pick up a fragment that is about the size of a marble. What type of tephra is it?

5. How are tephra bombs formed?

25

VOLCANOLOGIST ON DUTY

You've been up now for nearly 24 hours. Your attention is focused on a volcano that is erupting in front of you. You keep an eye on the computers and instruments around you. They tell you what is going on at the volcano. They make it possible for you to watch the eruption from the safety of this observatory. As a volcanologist, you study volcanoes like this one to understand more about how they work. What you learn will help you save lives.

FACTFILE

This volcano hasn't erupted for several hundred years. It was considered to be dormant (sleeping). Volcanoes are put into three classes:

- An active volcano is one that has erupted at least once during the last 10,000 years.

- A dormant volcano is active, but it hasn't erupted for several hundred years. It may show signs of activity such as escaping gas.

- An extinct volcano is one that hasn't erupted for at least 10,000 years. It is highly unlikely to erupt again.

This dormant volcano is located at Haleakala National Park in Hawaii. It doesn't show any signs of activity.

A volcano is a vent, or opening, in Earth's crust. It may be on land or underwater.

CRATER
Gases, ash, and cinders (fragments of hardened lava) are ejected from the crater. They form a cloud that rises above the volcano.

CHIMNEY
Magma mixes with gases from melted rock. It rises up the chimney (conduit).

LAVA
Magma is called lava once it reaches the surface.

SIDE VENT
Magma may branch off to erupt through a side vent, an opening in the side of the mountain.

CONE
Layers of old lava form the volcano cone.

GASES
Pressure from gases builds until it triggers an explosion.

MAGMA CHAMBER
Hot molten rock called magma is under pressure in a magma chamber below the volcano.

Q CHALLENGE QUESTIONS

The eruption is becoming more intense. You pick up your camera and watch through the lens as you take pictures.

1. You see the first signs of molten rock flowing down the mountain. What is molten rock called?

2. Where did the molten rock go between the magma chamber and surface?

3. What is in the cloud that is growing higher and higher above the volcano?

4. You live near an extinct volcano. Should you be worried about it erupting? Why or why not?

5. Before this eruption, the volcano was both active and dormant. Why?

VARIETIES OF VOLCANOES

You've collected all the data you need from the eruption. Now you're off to check on two other volcanoes. This trip will take you halfway around the world! You settle back in the plane and look out the window. The rugged land below you is a volcanic field, where much volcanic activity has taken place. You spot a cinder cone, and then another. You know this area well. You've explored several sections at ground level. Now you're getting a very different view as you look at it from the air.

FACTFILE

All last week you worked with a strato volcano. Now you are flying over cinder cones. Tomorrow you will be at a shield volcano. That's all three of the main types of volcanoes!

- **Shield:** large with sloping sides. It erupts more gently than other types of volcanoes. The lava is fluid and flows freely. The sides are built up as the lava hardens.

- **Cinder cone:** cone-shaped with steep sides. Hardened bits of lava land near the vent and build up the sides. Usually it has a bowl-shaped crater.

- **Strato (also called composite):** cone-shaped with steep sides. It gives off gases, ash, and fragments of rock. The sides are built of layers of lava, ash, and volcanic debris. These are the most common volcanoes on Earth's surface.

An active volcano may behave in a number of different ways. It may simply give off steam and other gases. It may or may not have a lava flow. It might be explosive – or not. Some volcanoes go from one behaviour to another during a period of activity. These are the most common types of eruptions, going from the calmest to the most violent.

- **Hawaiian:** produces a quiet flowing of thin, fluid lava. This volcano may erupt as a fountain.

- **Strombolian:** makes noisy short blasts at regular intervals. It spits out lava and all sizes of tephra. Tephra is solid rock material thrown into the air during an eruption. It may be fine volcanic ash, or large chunks of cooled lava. After spitting tephra, the volcano may produce thick, sticky lava.

- **Vulcanian:** often begins by blowing away part of the mountain. A series of loud explosions may follow for a few hours. Ash and tephra are blasted skyward at high speed and scattered widely. A dense ash cloud rises from the peak.

- **Vesuvian:** may last for days. Huge amounts of ash and gases are blasted out at several hundred km/h. An umbrella-shaped ash cloud rises high into the atmosphere. Ash and pumice fall to the ground over a wide area.

- **Pelean:** highly destructive. A blast of steam, gas, lava, and red-hot ash shoots from the volcano. Fiery lava falls back to the ground and travels downhill as fast as 160 km/h.

Q CHALLENGE QUESTIONS

1. What type of eruption is likely to come from a shield volcano?
2. How are the sides of a cinder cone built up?
3. How are the sides of a strato volcano built up?
4. What is tephra?
5. Which type of eruption is more violent, Strombolian or Pelean?

LAVA FLOWS

Your plane lands in Hawaii, and you quickly catch another flight. You are eager to get to the Big Island, and one of the most active volcanoes in the world! Kilauea, a shield volcano, has been erupting for more than 20 years. Recently, its lava flow has been increasing. Some local seismologists meet your flight. You jump into their van and head out to where the lava is slowly oozing across a road.

FACTFILE

- On the way, you see a fiery river of molten lava making its way down the slope.
- A large lava lake is taking shape in a valley. This is an unusual sight! The bright lava is forming a silver crust as it cools.
- Up near the summit, fire fountains of lava shoot into the air. Red-hot tephra rains down in a glowing curtain.

All types of lava are made of the same materials.

Lava consists mostly of silica, which is a combination of silicon and oxygen. Lava also contains iron, magnesium, potassium, calcium, and other elements.

There are four different types of lava. Each type is determined by the percentage of silica it contains. The higher the percentage of silica, the more slowly the lava flows.

Lava type	Silica
Basalt	45-52%
Andesite	52-63%
Dacite	63-68%
Rhyolite	More than 68%

Lava can also be described by the way that it flows and cools.

- **Pahoehoe lava** is thin and flows smoothly. It moves forward in globs that break out from under a cooled crust. Some pahoehoe lava looks like twisted ropes when it cools.

- **Aa lava** is thick and sticky. It flows more slowly. Its surface is rough with chunks of broken lava. When it cools, it is jagged and sharp enough to cut through your shoes!

- **Pillow lava** forms when molten lava comes into contact with water. As the lava cools, it forms mounds of pillow shapes. Pillow lava is the most common type of lava, because most volcanoes are near or under water.

Lava can be as hot as 1200° C. This lava isn't quite that hot, but its intense heat is enough to melt the pavement and cause trees to burst into flames!

Q CHALLENGE QUESTIONS

1. Which lava flows most easily? Why is this?
2. What would you call lava which is 64% silica?
3. What is silica made of?
4. What happens to lava when it erupts in water?
5. What type of lava is most common? Why?

GALWAY COUNTY LIBRARIES

VOLCANIC ISLAND

After several days of studying the lava flow, you are back on a plane again. This time you are heading for a volcano on an island in the Pacific Ocean. This volcano is classified as active, but it has been quiet for the last 60 years. Now it is showing signs that it is going to erupt soon! It has taken a couple of flights to get to this remote spot. You are almost there at last. You can see the volcano's distinctive cone shape rising above the dark blue ocean waters.

FACTFILE

- The VEI (Volcanic Explosivity Index) runs from 0 (low) to 8 (high). Most eruptions have a VEI between 0 and 5.
- The measurement of an eruption is based on several factors, including the height of the ash cloud and the amount of tephra.

VEI	Description of volcanic eruption	Height of the ash cloud	Average frequency
0	Non-explosive	Less than 100 metres	Daily
1	Gentle	100–1,000 metres	Daily
2	Explosive	1–5 kilometres	Weekly
3	Severe	3–15 kilometres	Yearly
4	Cataclysmic (overwhelmingly violent)	10–25 kilometres	10 years or more
5	Paroxysmal (suddenly, violently explosive)	over 25 kilometres	50 years or more
6	Colossal (huge)	over 25 kilometres	100 yrs+
7	Super-colossal	over 25 kilometres	1,000 yrs+
8	Mega-colossal	over 25 kilometres	10,000 yrs+

You wonder how the force of this volcano's eruption will measure up against other volcanoes on the Volcanic Explosivity Index:

Volcano	Unzen	Cerro Hudson	Mount Pinatubo
Location	Japan	Chile	Philippines
VEI	4	5	6
Eruption year	1990	1991	1991

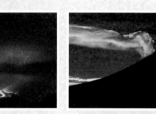

Volcano	Hekla	Ulawun	Reventador
Location	Iceland	Papua New Guinea	Ecuador
VEI	3	4	4
Eruption year	2000	2000	2002

Volcano	Galeras	Reventador	Cleveland
Location	Colombia	Ecuador	Alaska
VEI	3	2	3
Eruption year	2004	2004	2006

Q CHALLENGE QUESTIONS

1. Which volcano in the chart had the strongest eruption? What was its VEI?
2. How many of these eruptions had a VEI of 4 or more?
3. Which volcano erupted twice within two years?
4. Which volcanoes had the same VEI as Hekla in Iceland?
5. Which volcano had an 'explosive' eruption?

RING OF FIRE

Volcanologists and other scientists from all over the world have gathered at the island's laboratory. It's a busy place! All around the room, people are checking data and discussing the coming eruption. Some are comparing notes and making predictions. You join two other volcanologists who are studying a map. It shows the location of all the known active volcanoes in the world.

FACTFILE

Most volcanoes are located around the edges of Earth's tectonic plates. These are rigid sections of crust that float on top of magma in Earth's mantle. This diagram shows you what Earth is made up of:

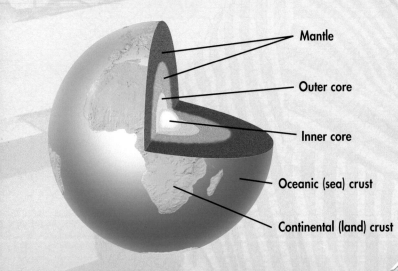

- Mantle
- Outer core
- Inner core
- Oceanic (sea) crust
- Continental (land) crust

Most volcanoes form along the edges of tectonic plates. That's where it's easiest for magma to push up towards the surface.

- There are 12 main tectonic plates and about 40 smaller ones. They fit together like a jigsaw puzzle.
- The plates are in constant slow motion, pushing together and pulling apart.
- As the plates move, magma seeps through the crust, forming a volcano.
- About 75% of the world's active and dormant volcanoes encircle the Pacific Ocean. This region is called the Ring of Fire.

This volcanologist is keeping an eye on a seismograph. It measures the shaking of the ground around the volcano.

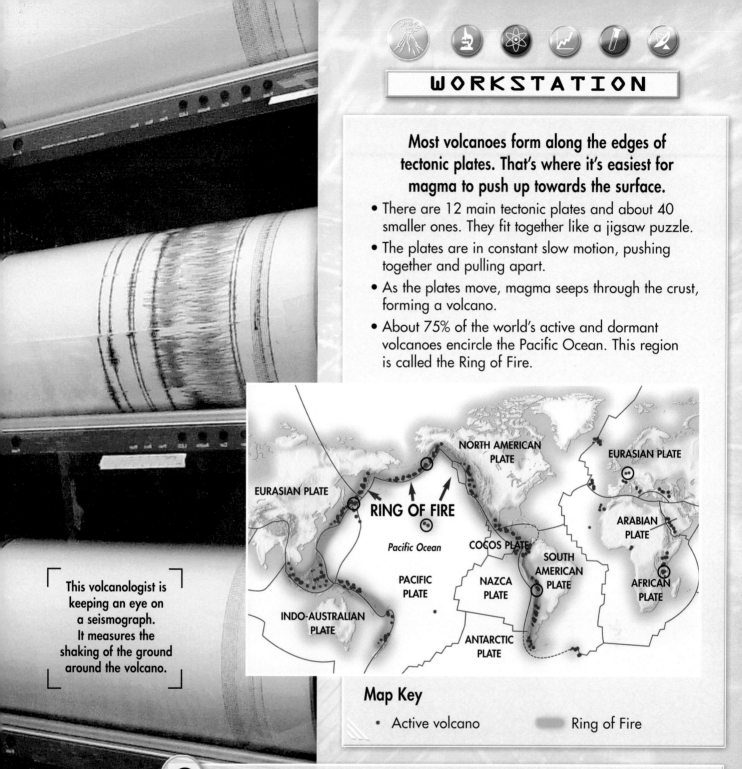

NORTH AMERICAN PLATE

EURASIAN PLATE

EURASIAN PLATE

RING OF FIRE

ARABIAN PLATE

Pacific Ocean

COCOS PLATE

SOUTH AMERICAN PLATE

AFRICAN PLATE

PACIFIC PLATE

NAZCA PLATE

INDO-AUSTRALIAN PLATE

ANTARCTIC PLATE

Map Key

• Active volcano   Ring of Fire

Q CHALLENGE QUESTIONS

One of the other volcanologists tells you that she has visited several other volcanoes so far this year. She circles their locations on a map.

1. How many volcanoes in the Ring of Fire did she visit?
2. Some of the circled volcanoes are not on boundaries. On which plates are they located?
3. What is a tectonic plate?
4. What does the movement of tectonic plates have to do with the formation of a volcano?
5. About what percentage of the world's active and dormant volcanoes are part of the Ring of Fire?

BULGE IN THE VOLCANO

There are different ways to tell when a volcano is close to erupting. A few days ago, you placed an electronic distance meter (EDM) on the volcano. Now it's time check the data it's been collecting. A helicopter takes you to near the base of the mountain, where the EDM is situated. You gather the information you need. The next stop is halfway up the mountain. You want to set up another instrument, called a tiltmeter.

You can see a bulge on the left of this volcano.

FACTFILE

Magma inside a volcano is under great pressure. As it rises, it puts pressure on the rock around it. It can cause the surface of the volcano to change in appearance. Deformation is a change in the height of the land around the volcano.

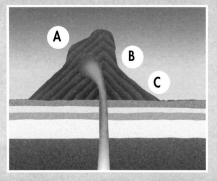

A. The changes may be large, such as a bulge in the volcano's side.

B. Sometimes an area on the sides may sink in.

C. Some changes are small, such as a slight difference in the tilt, or slope, of the land.

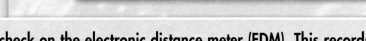

WORKSTATION

First you check on the electronic distance meter (EDM). This records changes in the surface of the volcano.

A volcanologist takes an EDM reading.

- EDMs are set up around the volcano to survey each side.
- The EDM aims a laser beam at a reflector on the side of the volcano. The beam is reflected back to the EDM. The EDM then calculates the angle of the slope.
- You compare data from the last several days. It shows that the angle of the ground has changed. This means that pressure from the rising magma has changed the shape of the volcano.

A scientist installs a tiltmeter on a volcano.

On the side of the volcano, you dig a hole for the tiltmeter.

- Tiltmeters are 'planted' in shallow holes in the ground to keep them in place.
- They record changes in the angle of the ground.
- Their data is passed as radio waves by a solar-powered instrument (transponder). The radio data is picked up by a passing satellite and sent to scientists at the observatory.

Q CHALLENGE QUESTIONS

During the last week, data from an EDM has been showing a growing bulge in the volcano's side.

1. What is causing the bulge?
2. Why are EDMs set up in several different locations?
3. What data would you expect to find from a tiltmeter stationed near the bulge?
4. Give one reason why the tiltmeter is partly buried, and not just sitting on the ground.
5. How does the data get from the tiltmeter to the laboratory?

RIGHT AT THE RIM

The helicopter has dropped you off near the crater. Gas and steam are rising out of the ground. You don't want to breathe these sulphurous gases. They are very bad for your health. Besides, one of them, hydrogen sulphide, smells like rotten eggs! The conditions for gathering gas samples are perfect today. The volcano seems calm, and the weather is good. You have a helicopter waiting in case the activity of the volcano starts to increase.

FACTFILE

All around you are volcanic gases. Water vapour (H_2O), carbon dioxide (CO_2), and sulphur dioxide (SO_2) are the most common.

- Volcanic gases are dissolved in the underground magma.
- They form bubbles and escape as the magma rises to the surface.
- They seep out through fumaroles, vents, and the ground.
- Some volcanic gases are poisonous. They can harm plants and animals several miles downwind.
- They may be released long before an eruption begins. Sometimes they continue for hundreds or thousands of years after it ends.

The gases and heat can kill trees.

Fumaroles are openings in the ground through which gases and steam escape.

A gas mask will protect you from breathing in dangerous gases.

As you collect gas samples, you are looking for changes in certain gases.

- As magma rises to the surface, different gases are released. This tells you that an eruption could happen soon!

There are several different ways to measure the contents of volcanic gas.

- Direct samples can be taken as gas escapes from the ground.

- Specially equipped planes and satellites can measure the gases in volcanic plumes.

- Measurements can be taken by automated equipment. The instruments are set up near an area where gases are escaping. Then they are left to run on their own.

- Samples of soil can show the levels of gases in the soil.

Q CHALLENGE QUESTIONS

1. Which method do you use to sample gases from a volcanic plume?
2. What are the three most common volcanic gases?
3. What are you looking for when you collect samples of volcanic gases?
4. Why should you wear a mask when collecting volcanic gases?
5. What is the advantage of using automated equipment?

SHAKY GROUND

You work your way back down the mountain a short distance. You are using a GPS (Global Positioning System) hand-held device. It guides you to the seismometer you are looking for. It's one of several placed at different locations on the volcano. A seismometer is an instrument that detects and records the shaking of the ground during an earthquake. You can look at a recorded pattern and tell the difference between various kinds of earthquakes – including those that show that a volcano is about to erupt.

Scientists check a buried seismometer on the side of a volcano.

FACTFILE

While you are on the mountain, you check on one other piece of equipment: the crackmeter.

- Sometimes the movement of the ground causes cracks to form.

- The crackmeter measures if the cracks are getting wider or narrower.

- The instrument consists of a bar held across the crack by anchors at each end driven into the ground.

- The width of the crack is measured by a gauge.

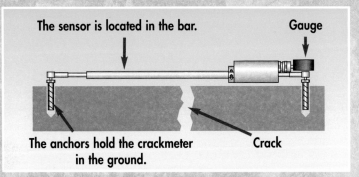

The sensor is located in the bar.   Gauge

The anchors hold the crackmeter in the ground.   Crack

The ground shakes slightly beneath your feet. Is it magma moving below, or perhaps a rockslide on the mountain?

- As magma moves underground, it pushes aside solid rock and causes the ground to shake. Shallow earthquakes usually take place both before and during the eruption of a volcano.

- The seismometer measures the shaking as electronic signals.

- The signals are sent to the laboratory, and printed. The printout is called a seismogram.

- The data can be analysed to learn the time, location, depth, and magnitude (strength) of the earthquake.

- The data from a seismometer can be used to track the movement of the magma underground.

You're back at the lab, looking at the seismograms from the last few weeks. There have been four different types of earthquakes:

Deep earthquakes that take place in Earth's crust. The vibrations start close together and spread out.

Shallow earthquakes that occur at the center of the volcano's crater. The tremors are large and spread out.

Surface movements, such as rockfalls and landslides. The vibrations start small, and become larger and larger.

Long-lasting rhythmic shakings that often take place around active volcanoes, called harmonic tremors.

J245,120

Q CHALLENGE QUESTIONS

1. How would you classify each of these seismograms?

A.

B.

C.

D.

2. What does the crackmeter measure?

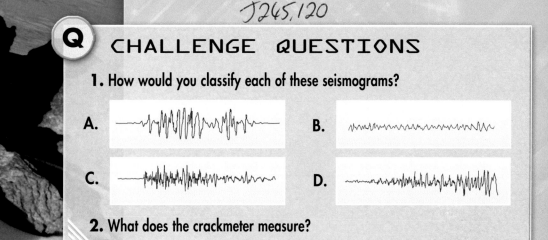

ERUPTION ALERT

Ever since the volcano started showing signs of erupting, the people living nearby have been on alert. Local officials have been urging people to leave. No one knows for definite what will happen to the villages on the island when the volcano erupts. Steam and gases are rising from the crater. The earthquakes are getting stronger. Even so, some people are still reluctant to leave their homes. You put out another warning: it is time to get everyone out – NOW!

The villagers are evacuated using any available vehicles.

FACTFILE

Many local residents have already decided to leave because of your warnings.

- A refugee center has been set up and is in operation now.

- A house-to-house search is being made to make sure that nobody has stayed behind.

- All roads towards the volcano are closed.

- An emergency search and rescue crew is on alert.

Rescue workers help to evacuate residents.

You are very concerned that the coming eruption will trigger a deadly mudflow called a lahar.

- A lahar is a thick mudflow made of water mixed with volcanic ash, rock, and mud.
- It looks like wet cement pouring down the slopes of a volcano.
- It can carry rock debris of all sizes, from tiny pieces of clay to boulders 10 metres across or more.
- A lahar can be hundreds of metres wide, flow as fast as 65 km/h, and travel as far as 80 kilometres.
- It can pick up more water and rock debris as it flows and grow to 10 times its original size.

This picture shows a mudflow caused by a volcano erupting in Colombia, in 1985. This mudflow completely destroyed a village.

A mudflow at the Galunggung Volcano, in Java, Indonesia, 1982.

There are various factors that could cause a lahar.

- It could be caused by the sudden melting of snow and ice during an eruption.
- The shaking of the ground might cause a section of the mountain to break loose in a landslide. Then the earth could slide into a river or lake, causing the water to spill over and start a lahar.
- Sometimes the movement of earth causes a lake to break out and spill.
- A heavy rain may start a lahar by washing away rock that was deposited or shaken loose during an eruption.

Q CHALLENGE QUESTIONS

1. Why is a house-to-house search necessary?
2. How can a lahar be caused by the heat of an eruption?
3. What materials are found in a lahar?
4. How could a lahar grow to 10 times its original size?
5. How fast can a lahar travel? How far?

EYEWITNESS TO AN ERUPTION

The eruption has started. It is stunning. You hold your breath as you watch. But you are also very busy working with the data as it comes in. The sights and sounds of the eruption surround you as you go about your work. You measure, record, and take pictures even as you are caught up in the spectacular events unfolding around you. Everyone in the lab will be very busy for a while.

FACTFILE

The volcano erupts with a huge blast.

- One side of the mountain collapses, releasing pressure.

- The natural dam of a lake cracks and then crumbles.

- A flood of water from the lake spills down the side of the mountain and mixes with hot ash. A lahar is set in motion.

- The lahar picks up rock debris as it races downhill, gaining speed.

Some buildings are carried away by the mudflow, while others are buried.

This volcano is blasting out a huge amount of tephra. The ash is rising and blowing away. The rest is raining down all around the volcano.

• Ash is the smallest kind of tephra. It ranges from very fine to rather coarse grains.

• Lapilli are fragments that are larger than a pea but smaller than a walnut. They look like cinders.

• Blocks are larger chunks of rock with angular sides. They were solid when they were blown out of the volcano.

• Bombs were molten lava when they were shot from the volcano. They cooled quickly as they flew through the air, so they have a rounded, streamlined shape.

• Tephra can be deadly. During and after an eruption, ash can fill the air, making it difficult to breathe. Some cities have been buried as much as three metres deep.

• Pumice is a volcanic rock. It is very light in weight because it is full of holes. The holes were formed by gases expanding as erupting lava cooled.

Q CHALLENGE QUESTIONS

Through the eruption, you take photographs. These will go in the lab's permanent records.

1. Which type of tephra is so small and light that it can ride the wind for hundreds of kilometres?

2. The volcano spits out jagged chunks of rock more than 30 centimetres wide. What type of tephra are they?

3. You find a chunk of volcanic rock which is so lightweight that it floats. What is it called?

4. You pick up a fragment that is about the size of a marble. What type of tephra is it?

5. How are tephra bombs formed?

ASH CLOUDS

When the eruption began, you watched as a column of hot ash burst with great force from the vent. In less than 10 minutes, it had risen more than 16 kilometres into the air. As it rose, it carried chunks of rock and cooling lava skyward, spitting them out in all directions. Now it is topped by a steadily growing ash cloud, also known as an eruption cloud or plume. You watch to see which direction the wind will carry the cloud.

> This ash cloud is a dark brownish-grey, although sometimes they are white or lighter grey.

FACTFILE

- During the eruption, steam and other expanding gases force material out of the vent.

- The ash column rises until it reaches a level where it is the same density as the surrounding air. Then it spreads out sideways to form a cloud. Leftover energy may cause it to rise a little further.

- Depending on the size of the eruption, an ash cloud may last minutes or months. However, it carries less tephra as time goes on.

The ash column usually travels straight up, but a strong wind can blow it sideways.

The pyroclastic flow can be one of the deadliest parts of an eruption.
However, not all eruptions cause a pyroclastic flow.

The pyroclastic flow rolls along the ground and in the air.

- Pyroclastic flow is a thick cloud of extremely hot volcanic gases, ash, and pieces of volcanic rock.
- A pyroclastic flow forms when an eruption column becomes too heavy and collapses. The flow rolls down the mountain, at speeds faster than 95 km/h.
- The temperature inside the flow may reach 650°C. It quickly covers an area of many square kilometres.
- Ash and volcanic rock form layers up to 18 metres deep.
- The flow strips trees from the hillsides, up to 10 kilometres away from the crater.
- As the pyroclastic flow continues rolling along, for the next few kilometres, the trees are knocked down and snapped in half.
- After that, for several more kilometres, the trees are left standing but are killed by the intense heat.

You and some of your colleagues study the measurements you have taken of the ash cloud, since the eruption started.

Time	09:00	10:00	11:00	12:00	13:00	14:00	15:00	16:00
Height (m)	0	1,500	2,300	2,800	3,000	3,800	4,400	4,600

Q CHALLENGE QUESTIONS

1. During which time period did the ash cloud rise fastest?
2. When did it start to slow down?
3. During which time period is it likely to carry the most tephra?
4. Why is pyroclastic flow so deadly?
5. What causes a pyroclastic flow to form?

ERUPTION AFTERMATH

As soon as it is safe to do so, you return to the village. It has been completely destroyed. You've seen the aftermath of an eruption many times, but you will never get used to the devastation. Still, there is some good news. Word has come from the refugee centre that everyone is safe. You think of other volcanic eruptions when thousands of people have been killed or injured. You are pleased to know that your efforts have helped the villagers to be safe.

> Everything, everywhere, is covered with a thick layer of fine grey ash. You see it, breathe it, and even taste it.

FACTFILE

You look around at the devastated landscape:

- Everything in sight is covered with fine grey ash.
- Flattened trees and burnt buildings show where the pyroclastic flow blasted through.
- A lahar has completely buried one side of the village.
- You can see the remains of a few houses. The rest are somewhere beneath all the mud and ash.

People are your first priority.

- These villagers need food, clothing, and shelter. Help will soon pour in from all over the world.

- Some villagers have developed health problems because of the ash in the air. They may have difficulty breathing, or have eye infections. A clinic will be set up to help these people.

- It may not be possible for these people to return to their village. The volcano could be active for years. You will advise them about building a new village in another location, away from the danger of the volcano.

At first, plants will not be able to grow in volcanic ash. But eventually the soil will become very fertile.

- Over time, the minerals in the ash break apart, and release nutrients like iron, magnesium and potassium into the soil.

- These nutrients are all important for the growth of plants, and make the soil fertile.

- One day forests will grow again where today you see only ash-covered ground.

This shoot is growing in volcanic ash.

Q CHALLENGE QUESTIONS

1. What effects did the pyroclastic flow have on the village?

2. Why should the villagers rebuild their homes in a different location?

3. What kind of health problems can be caused by ash?

4. What does volcanic ash do for the soil?

5. People often grow crops on the slopes of volcanoes. Why do you think this is?

GALWAY COUNTY LIBRARIES

TIPS FOR SCIENCE SUCCESS

Pages 6-7

Volcanologist on Duty

A volcano is either active or extinct. If it has erupted in the last 10,000 years, it's active. If it hasn't, it's extinct. What about an active volcano that hasn't erupted for a long time – even hundreds of years? That doesn't sound very active, does it? Such a volcano is said to be active but dormant, or 'sleeping.' It could erupt again!

Pages 8-9

Varieties of Volcanoes

Both strato volcanoes and cinder cones are cone-shaped. Both have steep sides. What's the difference between them? One big difference is the way their sides are built up. Check out the FACTFILE for that information.

You may have heard about a type of volcano called 'composite'. That's the same thing as a strato volcano. It's just a different name for it!

Pages 12-13

Volcanic Island

You'll find several different pieces of information in the WORKSTATION chart. It gives the name of the volcano, its location, and even an actual photograph. Be sure to pay attention to the eruption year. A couple of volcanoes are listed more than once. It's the same mountain, but different eruptions took place at different times!

Pages 14-15

Ring of Fire

There is a very close connection between volcanoes and earthquakes. Both are often the result of movement of tectonic plates. About 90% of the world's earthquakes take place along the Ring of Fire.

Pages 18-19

Right at the Rim

When a volcano is getting close to erupting, the amount of gases escaping may increase. Volcanologists are looking for something else when they collect gas samples. They want to find out what different types of gases are being given off. How are they mixed together? How concentrated are they? These things may change as the volcano gets closer to erupting.

Pages 20-21

Shaky Ground

No two seismograms from different earthquakes look exactly alike – even if they are records of the same type of earthquake. A volcanologist reading a seismogram is looking for patterns. Seismograms from the same type of earthquake will show some of the same patterns. There will also be some differences.

Pages 22-23

Eruption Alert

There's a good reason why a lahar looks like wet concrete as it flows. Concrete is made of finely ground mineral material, plus water, sand, and gravel or crushed stone. That's very much like the materials found in a lahar.

Pages 24-25

Eyewitness to an Eruption

Tephra categories are grouped according to size. Within each group are many different types. They may not look at all alike except for their size. They may be made of different materials or cooled in different ways.

Pages 26-27

Ash Clouds

Do the times given in the WORKSTATION chart look a bit unusual? Scientists don't always use our familiar 12-hour clock. A 24-hour way of recording time avoids confusion as to whether the event took place during the day or the night.

ANSWERS

Pages 6-7

1. Lava.
2. Through the conduit or chimney.
3. Gases, ash, and cinders.
4. No, because an extinct volcano is not likely ever to erupt again.
5. It had erupted at least once during the last 10,000 years, but it had been several hundred years since its last eruption.

Pages 8-9

1. Hawaiian.
2. Hardened bits of lava pile up around the vent.
3. They are formed from layers of lava, ash, and volcanic debris.
4. Solid rock material thrown up into the air during an eruption.
5. Pelean.

Pages 10-11

1. Basalt – it flows the most easily because it contains the least silica.
2. Dacite.
3. Silicon and oxygen.
4. It cools and forms into pillow shapes.
5. Pillow lava, because most volcanoes are near or under water.

Pages 12-13

1. Pinatubo; VEI-6.
2. Five – Unzen; Cerro Hudson; Pinatubo; Ulawun; and Reventador (2002).
3. Reventador in 2002 and 2004.
4. Galeras and Cleveland.
5. Reventador (2004).

Pages 14-15

1. Three.
2. On the Pacific, Eurasian, and African plates.
3. A rigid section of Earth's crust that floats on top of magma in Earth's mantle.
4. As the plates push together and pull apart, magma seeps through the crust and forms a volcano.
5. About 75%.

Pages 16-17

1. The magma rising inside the volcano is under great pressure. It pushes against the rock and causes it to bulge outward.
2. To survey each side of the volcano.
3. A difference in the angle (tilt) of the land.
4. The movement of the ground as the bulge forms could knock over the tiltmeter.
5. A transponder sends out radio waves. They are picked up by a satellite and transmitted to the observatory.

Pages 18-19

1. Aircraft and satellite measurement.
2. Water vapour (H_2O); carbon dioxide (CO_2); and sulphur dioxide (SO_2).
3. Changes in certain gases.
4. Some of the gases are dangerous to breathe.
5. It can be left to run on its own – no one needs to be around for it to do its work.

Pages 20-21

1. A. Shallow earthquake.
   B. Harmonic tremor.
   C. Deep earthquake under Earth's crust.
   D. Surface movement, such as a landslide or rockfall.
2. The crackmeter measures the width of cracks caused by the movement of the ground.

Pages 22-23

1. To be sure that no one has stayed behind.
2. The heat causes snow and ice on the volcano to melt quickly. The water flows down the mountain, mixing with ash and mud.
3. Water, volcanic ash, rock, and mud.
4. The lahar can pick up more water and rock debris as it flows.
5. 65 km/h; up to 80 kilometres.

Pages 24-25

1. Ash.
2. Blocks.
3. Pumice.
4. Lapilli.
5. They begin as molten lava and cool off as they fly through the air.

Pages 26-27

1. 9:00am–10:00am.
2. 12pm.
3. 9:00am–10:00am.
4. It is extremely hot and moves quickly.
5. The eruption column becomes heavy and collapses.

Pages 28-29

1. It knocked down trees and burnt houses.
2. They need to find a place that would be safer.
3. Ash may cause eye infections and problems with breathing.
4. The volcanic ash makes the soil more fertile.
5. Volcanic soil becomes very fertile, and makes good farmland.

GLOSSARY

ASH CLOUD Gases, ash, and rock fragments that have risen into the atmosphere during a volcanic eruption; also known as an eruption cloud or plume.

BASALT A fine-grained, dark-coloured volcanic rock.

CINDERS Volcanic rock fragments that form from gas-filled lava thrown into the air. The lava becomes solid as it falls.

CRATER A steep-sided, usually bowl-shaped pit at the summit of a volcano. It is formed by either an explosion or a collapse at the vent.

DEBRIS Broken pieces of rock.

DEFORMATION A change in the shape of a material, caused by pressure, strain, or stress.

ERUPTION COLUMN Hot volcanic ash ejected during an eruption that forms the lower, usually vertical, part of the ash cloud.

FUMAROLE A volcanic vent through which volcanic gases escape.

GLOBAL POSITIONING SYSTEM (GPS) A navigation system which uses satellites to give a precise location.

LAHAR A type of mudflow that begins on the side of a volcano when water, volcanic ash, and other debris combine and flow rapidly downhill.

MAGNITUDE A measurement of the energy released during an earthquake.

MINERAL A solid non-organic material, which can be found in nature.

NUTRIENT A substance which helps living creatures grow and gives them energy.

OBSERVATORY A building designed for observing something and taking measurements.

PRESSURE The force of two things pressing against each other.

PYROCLASTIC FLOW An extremely hot mixture of ash, gas, and volcanic rock fragments that travels at high speed down the sides of a volcano or along the surface of the ground.

SEISMOGRAM The printed record of information recorded by a seismograph.

SEISMOGRAPH An instrument that makes a record of the vibrations caused by an earthquake.

SEISMOMETER An instrument that measures the vibrations of Earth at a specific location.

SULPHUROUS GASES Gases that contain the element sulphur (S).

TECTONIC PLATES Rigid sections of Earth's crust that float on top of the magma in Earths's mantle.

TEPHRA Rock materials of all sizes that are thrown into the air during an eruption.

TRANSPONDER A wireless communication instrument that picks up an incoming signal and automatically sends it to another location.

VENT An opening at Earth's surface through which volcanic materials erupt.

VOLCANIC FIELD An area of Earth's crust containing several volcanoes.

PICTURE CREDITS

l=left, r=right, t=top, c=centre, b=bottom

Alamy: 16-17 (main), 16-17(main), 22-23(main). Corbis: ofc, obc tl, obc br, 1, 6-7(main) Bettmann/CORBIS, 10-11, 10b, 13tl, 18-19 (main), 22b Reuters/CORBIS, 24-25 (main), 24b, 25ct, 25cb, 28b Reuters/CORBIS, 30-31(main), 30l, 32 (main). Getty: 13cl, 13c, 14-15(main) Dinodia Picture Agency, 29t AFP/Getty, 28-29(main) AFP/Getty. iStockPhoto: 2t, 25t. NOAA: 13bl. Oregon State University: 19b. Photoatlas: 13bc. Rex Features: 23tr. Science Photo Library: 8-9 (main), 19t, 20-21 (main), 23cl W.K. Fletcher/Science Photo Library, 27t. Shutterstock 6c iofoto, 11t, 11b, 12-13 (main), 16b Lisa F. Young, 19ct, 26-27(main). Still Pictures: 29c H. Baesemann/Still Pictures. USGS: 8t, 8c, 8b, 13tr, 17t, 17c, 18c, 18b, 19cb, 26b. ticktock media archive: 7c, 9ft, 9t, 9c, 9b, 9fb, 14b, 15c, 16b, 20b Wikimedia: 11c, 13tc, 13cr, 13br, 25b.

Every effort has been made to trace the copyright holders, and we apologise in advance for any unintentional omissions. We would be pleased to insert the appropriate acknowledgments in any subsequent edition of this publication.

GALWAY COUNTY LIBRARIES